Original title:
Arbor's Anthem

Copyright © 2025 Creative Arts Management OÜ
All rights reserved.

Author: Nathaniel Blackwood
ISBN HARDBACK: 978-1-80567-266-1
ISBN PAPERBACK: 978-1-80567-565-5

Melodies of Mossy Monuments

In the woods where the trees dance and sway,
The squirrels throw parties all night and day.
With acorns as hats and leaves for their shoes,
They laugh at the owls with their wise, grumpy blues.

The roots play a jingle, a rooty old tune,
While mushrooms groove under the light of the moon.
The branches all sway, making quite the parade,
As critters join in, no one's ever dismayed.

The bushes are bouncing with berries so bright,
They gossip and giggle, causing such a fright.
The pine cones are clapping, it's quite a sight,
As the saplings form conga lines, pure delight.

So if you should wander where the tallies grow,
Remember the fun and the laughter they throw.
With nature's own choir and a mossy embrace,
The forest is laughing, a joyous place.

A Canopy of Connection

Under leafy boughs, we sway in delight,
Squirrels debating, who's taking the bite.
A branch full of laughter, we shake with glee,
While roots giggle softly, beneath the big tree.

The sun plays a game, peek-a-boo with our shade,
While acorns drop down, like confetti, parades!
With whispers of breezes, that tickle our toes,
We dance with the flowers, where anything grows.

Songs from the Soil

In the dirt we discover, the tunes of the ground,
Worms humming softly, a wiggly sound.
With boots like percussion, we stomp and we hop,
As daisies join in, they just can't stop!

The beetles bring rhythm, the ants keep in line,
As daisies and dandelions all intertwine.
With laughter that bubbles, and roots that rejoice,
Each blossom a note in our nature's choice.

The Murmurs of Moss

On a log, soft and cozy, the moss starts to speak,
Whispering secrets that only we seek.
It chuckles and laughs, with a foresty cheer,
Inviting the faeries to come and draw near.

Each tiny green tuft, a tale to unfold,
Of dreams in the rain, and adventures bold.
With a giggle from puddles, and a sigh from the shade,
Life under the canopy, is never delayed.

Chords of the Canopy

Up high in the branches, the ukuleles play,
With melodies sweet, that brighten the day.
The wind makes us dance, as the leaves join the song,
In this silly concert, where all of us belong.

With a strum of the bark, and a hum from the bees,
Nature's orchestra plays, while we sway in the breeze.
We cheer for the owls, the conductors of night,
As stars join the chorus, oh, what a sight!

Sonnet of the Shimmering Leaves

Breezes tickle leaves on high,
Squirrels practice acrobatic fly.
Tree trunks wear hats made of moss,
While branches gossip like a boss.

In the shade, ants have a parade,
Chasing crumbs in a bright charade.
Birds chirp tunes that make us smile,
Nature's comic relief, full of style.

Ballet of the Sun-dappled Path

Sunshine twirls like a little dancer,
Paths sprout flowers, like a prancer.
Bugs buzzing, choreographing delight,
While turtles start their slow-motion flight.

Rabbits hop in fanciful spritz,
Playing tag, oh, what a blitz!
Leaves sway gently, waving hands,
In this woodland, joy expands.

Twilight in the Timber Enclave

Evening glows, fireflies in a race,
Mice throw cheese parties, quite the place!
Owls joke about who hoots the best,
While crickets serenade the nest.

The raccoons wear masks, ready to steal,
Midnight feasts, they spin the wheel.
Branches creak, sharing old tales,
Of mischievous winds and silly gales.

Journeys Through Green Forays

Wandering through the leafy maze,
Adventures hidden in nature's gaze.
Frogs in sunglasses take a leap,
While whispers in the bushes keep.

The laughter of trees fills the air,
Each trunk boasts, trying to compare.
Roots play tag, squirming on ground,
Joined by mushrooms, round and profound.

Whispers of the Waving Willows

The willows giggle in the breeze,
Their branches tickle all with ease.
A squirrel darts, a bird's in flight,
They plan their party for the night.

With leafy hats and twinkling lights,
They dance around till morning's heights.
A picnic spread with acorn pies,
The willows laugh, the sun will rise!

Symphony of the Leafy Canopy

In a choir of leaves, the trees unite,
Singing songs of silly fright.
A cat climbs high, a dog looks up,
They wonder who will sing the cup!

The melody flows with rustling cheer,
To every critter, far and near.
A parrot squawks a funny tune,
As branches sway beneath the moon.

The Roots Beneath Our Soles

Roots may twist and roots may shout,
While creatures stomp and dance about.
They wiggle underfoot with glee,
Holding secrets, deep and free.

A worm pops up; "Hey, what's the fuss?"
While ants march by, they make a fuss.
The earth chuckles, "Don't you know?
We're just here for the tree-top show!"

Crescendo of the Evergreen

The pines are plotting quite a game,
To trick the maples with their name.
"Evergreen's the best," they boast,
While birches laugh and plot a roast.

They gather round for tales of yore,
With cones for hats and laughter galore.
A breeze arrives; they start to sway,
In their green gowns, they dance and play.

Beneath Canopy Dreams

In the shade where squirrels play,
Each acorn's a treasure, on display.
A rabbit hops, wearing a hat,
Chasing the sun while dodging the cat.

Under the leaves, I find my seat,
With ants in a march, we dance to the beat.
The wind whispers jokes with a playful wink,
As petals confetti, in colors they think.

Leaves in Lyrical Motion

The leaves twist and twirl in the breeze,
They gossip like friends, oh such a tease!
A songbird croons, sounding quite bold,
With a chorus above that never gets old.

Each branch bends low, a wave of delight,
In the sunlight they shimmer, what a sight!
Bouncing from limb, a frog joins the fun,
He croaks out a tune, oh what a run!

Echoes of the Old Oak

The old oak chuckles, wise and round,
With tales of the past, its voice is profound.
It tells of a time when branches were young,
When trees dreamed of songs that had never been sung.

An owl in spectacles reads poetry at night,
With fireflies dancing, what a splendid sight!
The roots wiggle softly, a ticklish affair,
Waving at critters from here to there.

Treetop Serenade

Up high in the branches, a concert begins,
With a flutist beetle who surely has fins.
A raccoon strums, on a guitar made of bark,
While the moonlight winks in the velvet dark.

The leaves clap along, a rustling cheer,
As shadows of rabbits hop ever near.
The show goes on with a whimsy so grand,
Nature's own band, oh isn't it grand?

Dancing with Dappled Light

In the forest, shadows sway,
Squirrels spin in bright array.
Leaves chuckle as they twist and twirl,
Sunbeams giggle, watch them whirl.

Breezes tickle, rustle through,
Nature's dance, a funny view.
Mice in hats, do pirouettes,
Frogs in tuxedos place their bets.

Branches bow with graceful flair,
Treetop parties without a care.
Dancing shadows weave a tale,
Of woodland whims that never fail.

So grab a friend and come partake,
In this funny forest wake.
With dappled light and laughter wild,
Join the fun like nature's child.

Melodies Among the Branches

Birds performing, quite a show,
Singing tunes that steal the glow.
Chirps and twitters, what a sound,
In this leafy stage, joy is found.

Rabbits tap their tiny feet,
Beetles keep the rhythmic beat.
With every note the trees do sway,
A symphony of green ballet.

Whimsical winds through branches weave,
Tickling leaves that dance and cleave.
Nature's band, a riotous spree,
Conducted by a dancing bee.

Join the fun, don't be a stranger,
In this concert, fear no danger.
Underneath the sky so blue,
Let the melodies guide you through.

Guardians of the Green

Tree stumps gossip, roots collide,
Watch out, there goes a bushy ride!
With eyes that twinkle, leaves look down,
Guardians grin, in green they're crowned.

Raccoons in capes, they take a stand,
Fighting for the forest land.
With acorn helmets and barky shields,
They croon about their leafy fields.

Their battle cry, a joyful quack,
The trees can't help but laugh back.
With leafy laughter all around,
Nature's heroes can be found.

So raise a toast to those who cheer,
Our leafy guards, let's hold them dear.
With every rustle, join the scene,
In the kingdom of the evergreen.

The Embrace of the Elder Tree

The elder tree's a wobbly friend,
With branches low, they never end.
Critters nestle, all they crave,
In that cozy, leafy cave.

Squirrels play a game of chase,
With acorns as their favorite base.
The elder shakes, but does not fall,
Holding laughter, big and small.

Roots as arms, they hug so tight,
Crickets fiddle through the night.
Twirling shadows, sparkles bright,
Beneath the tree, a silly sight.

So give a shout, don't hold it in,
Join the glee where roots begin.
In the embrace of this wise old sage,
We find our joy, a playful stage.

The Breath of the Boughs

The branches stretched out wide, so free,
They tickle the clouds, oh what a spree!
Squirrels juggle nuts up in the trees,
While birds play tunes with wobbly knees.

The leaves gossip soft with a rustling cheer,
Whispering secrets only the squirrels hear.
A raccoon wears glasses, reading a book,
While bees buzz around with a curious look.

With each playful swing in a breezy swoosh,
The trunks break out dancing, oh what a woosh!
The sun beams laughter, casting long shadows,
As the forest joins in with funny meadows.

In the shade of the trees, we gather round,
For tickling ferns and laughter abound.
Nature's own comedy, the boughs all agree,
Singing and swinging so whimsically.

The Spirit of the Sapwood

In the realm of the trees, where giggles unfold,
Sapwood's no hero, but he's brave and bold.
He tells grand tales of a branch gone awry,
Of a squirrel who attempted to leap to the sky.

The knots twist and tumble, like dancers at play,
As shadows play tricks, then scamper away.
A pinecone circus with acorns in tow,
Unruly and raucous, but putting on a show.

The woodpecker drums with an upbeat refrain,
While the raccoons gather for a wild campaign.
They plot to steal snacks from the picnic nearby,
But trip over roots with a flop and a sigh.

In the heart of the forest, the laughter rings loud,
Flexing their branches, they stand oh-so-proud.
For in every twist of the wood there's a joke,
And the spirit of sapwood just loves to provoke.

Chronicles Under the Cénit

Under the sky where the sun likes to play,
Trees chuckle softly at the end of the day.
The chipmunk's a spy, with a nut in his stash,
Peeking from behind with a mischievous flash.

The oaks hold court, with their wisdom profound,
While vines tell the stories that twist all around.
A weasel slips by with a swift little grin,
Scribbling the tales where the fun must begin.

When night casts its veil, the critters get bold,
In shadows they frolic, a sight to behold.
The moon shines a spotlight on antics galore,
Of trees trading quips and old legends of yore.

The tales of the woods bloom under the stars,
Where laughter resounds, echoing from afar.
In the chronicles sung by the leaves of each tree,
Every twig tells a tale, every root holds a key.

The Glorious Glade

In the glade where the flowers trot in a line,
Sunbeams gleefully dance, oh so divine.
The daisies are jaunty, the lilies take flight,
Planning a party that lasts through the night.

The mushrooms will feast with a garlic parade,
While frogs do the cha-cha in a green masquerade.
A butterfly joins, spreading humor in style,
With each flippy flap, she brings forth a smile.

Bumblebees bumble, with plans of a brew,
Mixing sweet honey, just a drop or two.
The trees form a choir, with branches held high,
As the wind sings along, and the clouds just sigh.

So gather, dear friends, in the glade's warm embrace,
Where joy leaps through flowers, each livened space.
With laughter and glee all around in full bloom,
In nature's own circus, there's never a gloom.

The Lullaby of Larches

In the land where trees can chatter,
Larches giggle, leaves a-flatter.
Squirrels dance, their tails on show,
Waves of green in gentle flow.

Breeze will tickle branches bright,
Sunbeams laugh in pure delight.
All the critters join the fun,
Whispering tales 'til day is done.

O birds, do sing your silly song,
While roots and vines play along.
A forest full of joyful sights,
Sharing smiles beneath the heights.

So gather 'round, you woodland friends,
Here's where all the fun never ends.
With every leaf that flutters free,
Nature hums in harmony!

Serenading Shadows

In the park where shadows play,
Silly rabbits hop and sway.
They waltz beneath the old oak tree,
With every leap, they shout with glee.

The shadows stretch and then they prance,
As squirrels frolic, join the dance.
The moonbeam giggles and takes a turn,
While fireflies light the night and burn.

Here, the deer whisper silly dreams,
As hedgehogs snicker, or so it seems.
A raccoon yawns, oh what a sight,
Serenading all through the night.

Laughter echoes in the glade,
For every creature, a parade.
Let the trees bear witness too,
To every giggle, bright and true!

The Ode of the Old-growth

Oh, towering giants, wise and grand,
With branches that share jokes so unplanned.
In their bark, old whispers dwell,
Each ring a secret, a story to tell.

The owl hoots a riddle or two,
While woodpeckers play peek-a-boo.
And all the creatures, with hearts so light,
Gather around by the warm moonlight.

Fallen leaves drop, a confetti rain,
As chipmunks giggle, feeling no pain.
The fragrance of laughter fills the air,
In this sacred grove, joy is everywhere.

Let us toast to the quirky old trees,
Who sway and dance with every breeze.
In their arms, we find such cheer,
A symphony of nature, loud and clear!

Ink of the Earth

With roots like pens, they write the tales,
Of every creature that skips and wails.
A squirrel's antics, a deer's swift flight,
All painted in colors so warm and bright.

The soil, it chuckles, as flowers bloom,
While grasses sway and dance in plume.
Mushrooms giggle beneath the shade,
A playful world that laughter made.

Puddles splash with a joyous beat,
As frogs compose their hop-happy feat.
Each drop a story, a silly quirk,
In the quiet woods, where none can lurk.

So let us pen our tales so true,
In ink of the earth, a vibrant hue.
With each word written, joy takes flight,
In the boundless book of day and night!

Secrets in the Shaded Grove

In the grove, the whispers play,
Squirrels chat while stealing hay.
Leaves gossip about the sun,
Whirling tales of moonlit fun.

Beneath the boughs where shadows twirl,
A raccoon spins, giving a whirl.
Old roots chuckle, tickling toes,
As the breeze dances with the crows.

Every branch has stories grand,
Of silly critters in this land.
The grass laughs at a toppled snail,
"Keep it up, you'll surely fail!"

So, let's sing and sway our hearts,
In the grove where laughter starts.
With every twist and every bend,
Nature's joy will never end.

When the Bark Breathes Life

When the bark takes a deep breath,
Does it sigh for a life, or death?
Or perhaps it chuckles and beams,
As it stretches in sunlit dreams.

The snail yawned, "What's all this fuss?"
While ants held a meeting just for us.
With each ring, trees tell their tales,
Of secret lovers and wind-blown gales.

Do mushrooms gossip, or keep it hush?
Underneath where the gophers rush?
In the quiet, there's laughter and cheer,
As owls wink and toss back a beer.

Just imagine a tree that could chat,
It would crack jokes — just picture that!
With each creak and groan, it's a show,
Life in the woods is a curious flow.

Dance of the Branching Shadows

In the dusk when the shadows stretch,
Branches sway, a dance to fetch.
The moon takes the lead, the stars behind,
Whipping up a rhythm so kind.

Squirrels lead with leaps and bounds,
While rabbits stomp to leafy sounds.
A raccoon brings his ukulele,
Singing tunes that make us all waily.

The wind joins in with a playful twist,
Tickling leaves, waving to the mist.
Every rustle and chirp a song,
In this party, you can't go wrong!

So, let's twirl under the grand design,
Where shadows dance and all's divine.
In the twilight, joy leaps and sings,
As nature dons her party wings.

Echoes of the Canopy's Heart

In the thick of leaves, secrets hum,
Canopy's heart plays on a drum.
Each rustle a giggle, each sway a grin,
Nature's laughter, where fun begins.

A woodpecker thumps like a drummer's beat,
While butterflies dance on their tiny feet.
"Oh, what's that?" a chipmunk peeps,
"Just the world's laughter, it never sleeps!"

With critters sharing their daily plight,
In tales of woe that turn out light.
Here, mischief blooms on every branch,
As creatures frolic, daring a chance.

So hear the echoes, join the fun,
In this leafy world under the sun.
Where every whisper and chuckle praise,
The joy of life in leafy maze.

Ballad of the Verdant Veil

The trees sing whispers, quite absurd,
Branches bending, strokes unheard.
Squirrels dance with acorn hats,
Chasing shadows, like silly sprats.

A leaf fell down, took a spin,
Landed on a snail with a grin.
'Come join the party!' it proclaimed loud,
While mushrooms cheered, all so proud.

Beneath the bark, a wise old bug,
Shared tales of sap and a friendly slug.
"Honestly," he said with glee,
"I think I'm growing a maple tree!"

The sun peeked through in a jolly flare,
The branches juggled with utmost care.
Nature's circus, what a sight!
In this green realm, all feels just right.

Interlude at the Forest's Edge

At the forest's edge, a picnic spread,
Ants brought napkins, not a shred.
A raccoon borrowed some fine cheese,
While the owls napped in the cool breeze.

The frogs held a concert, quite a show,
Croaking rhythms, stealing the flow.
They claimed, 'Tonight, we'll croak a tune!'
While the crickets fiddled under the moon.

An argument sparked 'bout a mud pie,
As the turtles debated who's spry.
In a race that was rather slow,
That's when the rabbits put on a show!

With hats made of leaves and tails so proud,
They leapt and twirled, catching a crowd.
The forest echoed with laughter and cheer,
Ah, the wild times shared in the year!

Chronicles of the Rooted Realm

In the rooted realm, where giggles grow,
Beneath old oaks, a quirky show.
With gnarled hands, the roots will play,
At storytelling night, come what may!

The wise old tree claimed he's seen it all,
From acorn dreams to a squirrel's fall.
"I once was a mighty, mighty seed,
Just like you, with many a need!"

A gust of wind then chimed in bold,
"Hey, I'm the reason all tales are told!"
And the bushes rustled, wishing to drift,
With laughter that felt like the best gift.

So gather 'round, oh friends, and hear,
The roots tell secrets year after year.
In splendid antics, they never tire,
In this rich land, where legends conspire.

Serenade for the Swaying Silhouettes

Swaying silhouettes dance in delight,
With shadows that twirl in the pale moonlight.
A raccoon strummed a melodious tune,
While fireflies sparkled like stars in June.

The bushes giggled, prancing around,
Echoing laughter, a jubilant sound.
Each leaf would whisper a quirky jest,
To entertain all who came, quite blessed.

A stash of pinecones, like treasures found,
Held court for the critters on soft, mossy ground.
"What's the best way," one asked with a grin,
"To eat mushrooms without feeling thin?"

With merriment swirling, the night rolled on,
From dusk until the early dawn.
In this grand haven, where joy's the goal,
The swaying silhouettes captured each soul!

The Silent Strength of Ancient Boughs

Underneath the mighty limbs,
A squirrel plots with stealthy whims.
Whispers float as breezes blow,
Those ancient trees, they surely know.

With roots as deep as grandma's tales,
They hold their ground, despite the gales.
But watch out for the woodpecker's knock,
He's just asking for a chat—what a shock!

The trunks stand tall, all wise and stout,
Sending vibes of strength throughout.
Yet in the shade, a picnic sprawls,
While branches chuckle, "Tea's on the walls!"

So lift your glass to bark and leaf,
Amidst the green, there's joy and grief.
For every twig has laughter too,
As trees conspire—who knew they'd brew?

In Celebration of the Tall Giants

Oh, how they stretch and stand so proud,
Giant beacons, drawing a crowd.
With leafy crowns and roots that bind,
They dance on hills as wind unwinds.

In their shade, we picnic with glee,
"Who stole my sandwich?" we plea with esprit.
Eavesdropping on birds, they twist and twirl,
While ants march by like kings of the world.

Oh mighty friends, so tall and bright,
You keep us cool in the summer light.
Yet when the storms rumble and roar,
It's those tall giants we all adore!

Let's raise a toast to trunks so wide,
With laughter echoing, side by side.
For every tree holds secrets tight,
And shares them softly in the night.

Harmony in the Forest's Embrace

In the woods where laughter reigns,
The critters dance on leafy planes.
Moles are here throwing a ball,
While owls hoot, "Let's have a ball!"

Branches sway like a festive cheer,
And every rustle says, "Come near!"
The mushrooms giggle, all in line,
As sunlight spills its golden wine.

Frogs croak out their serenades,
While trees join in with leafy parades.
Even the fox, with mischief in mind,
Plays tag with shadows, so unconfined.

In this embrace, all feel so free,
A symphony from every tree.
Nature's joke, a silly game,
Let's laugh together; we're all the same!

The Lullaby of the Rustling Foliage

Hear the leaves, a soft parade,
Singing tunes, their serenade.
They whisper secrets, oh so deep,
Lulling all creatures, "Come take a leap!"

Boughs sway gently, oh what a sight,
As critters snuggle in for the night.
The breeze tickles, a playful tease,
And wraps us warm, like a hug from trees.

Chirping crickets join the song,
While fireflies dance the night along.
Each fluttering leaf, a silly jest,
In nature's arms, we laugh the best.

So nestle close in this leafy bed,
Whispers of trees, sweetly said.
Together we dream, with joy we weave,
In this nightly dance, we truly believe!

The Legacy of Leafy Legends

In a grove where squirrels plot,
The acorns scheme and twist a lot.
They hold debates about the breeze,
While critters laugh and munch with ease.

The owls hoot loudly in their style,
While trees just sway and grin awhile.
Each branch whispers secrets of lore,
As leaves join in a leafy roar.

Beneath the shade, a gnome awaits,
Trading tales with talking plates.
They banter 'bout the world above,
In their funny, woodland love.

So raise a toast to roots and bark,
For in this place, there's always spark.
With laughter in the gentle breeze,
Legacy lives with utmost ease.

Ponderings in the Pavilion of Pines

In a pavilion of piney dreams,
Squirrels argue 'bout the best ice creams.
One claims chocolate, another mint,
While branches bob and even squint.

A woodpecker drums a cheeky beat,
As roots sway and wiggle their feet.
The sun chuckles through leafy seams,
Lighting up their evergreen schemes.

Fragrant breezes bust a move,
While pondering all that nature could prove.
A rabbit jokes about the rain,
While shimmering leaves sing sweet refrain.

In this merry woodland plot,
Laughter's the best prize, it's got a lot.
With every pine and playful sound,
Joyful ponderings spin round and round.

The Founding Fig

In the land where the Fig once stood,
He pondered how to be more good.
He donned a hat made from a leaf,
Joking that he wore it as a chief.

With fruit so ripe, he ruled the way,
As bees and ants came out to play.
He claimed his reign was sweet and grand,
With sticky fingers, he made his stand.

"I declare this orchard full of fun,
Let's dance with shadows, everyone!"
The breeze chimed in with playful cheer,
As laughter echoed, far and near.

So raise a toast to the founding Fig,
Who fancied himself quite the bigwig.
In every fruit, a story thrives,
Of laughter, fun, and fruity lives.

The Scent of Science and Service

In a lab beneath a willow wide,
Scientists giggle, full of pride.
They mix up scents from leaves and soil,
Creating potions in their toil.

With test tubes clinking, frogs jump high,
As theories soar and laughter flies.
"Why did the tree join the debate?"
"Because it wanted to accumulate!"

They measure sap and count the bark,
While fireflies dance and leave a mark.
With each odd scent and bubbling spree,
They concoct fun as wild as can be.

In this blend of service and jest,
Nature's quirks put to the test.
With stories woven in the air,
Science laughs without a care.

Rhythms of the Swaying Pines

In the forest, pines do jig,
With a wiggle and a gig,
They laugh at squirrels in a race,
While mocking their acorn chase.

Branches twist in joyous flair,
Dancing lightly through the air,
Woodpeckers drum a silly beat,
As the sun taps tiny feet.

Breezes blow a cheeky tune,
To the light of the bright moon,
Shadows sway in playful games,
While all the trees call out names.

Laughter echoes, rich and wide,
In this leafy, verdant ride,
Nature's party, come and see,
Where fun has roots in every tree.

Voices of the Enchanted Glade

Frogs are croaking opera's song,
While crickets chirp all night long,
Even owls give a hoot or two,
They've got a choir, just for you.

Rabbits tap dance on the grass,
Inviting all the critters past,
With a wiggle and a hop,
They twirl until they drop.

The fireflies sparkle with delight,
Like little stars that feel just right,
In this glade, the fun won't cease,
As critters party, never cease.

Voices mingle, loud and sweet,
Nature's joy, a rhythmic beat,
Join the revelry, don't delay,
In this glade, we laugh and play.

Beneath the Blossoms' Gentle Embrace

Blossoms bloom in a soft parade,
While bees train for a sweet charade,
With petals swirling all around,
They form a band, without a sound.

Bunnies peek with curious eyes,
Amidst the flowers, oh what a surprise,
A dogwood tickles with a breeze,
While petals dance with leafy ease.

Grasshoppers play leapfrog at dawn,
While sunflowers yawn and stretch long,
Under blossoms, laughter grows,
As nature hums its funny prose.

In this place, joy fills the air,
With playful whispers everywhere,
Join the fun beneath the leaves,
Where every heart takes joy and weaves.

The Call of the Whispering Woods

In the woods, the trees all chat,
Spilling secrets, just like that,
Squirrels giggle, running fast,
Their chitter-chatter sure can last.

Branches sway with tales to tell,
Knots and gnarls know all too well,
The whispers carry on the breeze,
With stories told among the trees.

A raccoon shares a clumsy dance,
While shadows sway as if in trance,
With mossy benches inviting us,
To giggle, laugh, and sit nonplussed.

Join the chorus, hear the play,
Where the woods invite you to stay,
In the whispers, life is fun,
Nature's joke has just begun.

Stanzas of the Swaying Boughs

Leaves whisper jokes in the breeze,
Branches dance, bending with ease.
Squirrels giggle, chase their tails,
While the wise old oak tells tales.

A pine tree sways with a sneaky grin,
Hiding acorns, ready to win.
The wind takes a poke at the shady crew,
And the maples blush in vibrant hue.

The Allure of the Arboreal

Underneath the leafy embrace,
Bugs throw parties, a buzzing race.
Morning glories wear clownish hats,
As critters wander, sharing laughs and chats.

A beaver boasts of his dam so grand,
While a raccoon juggles rocks in hand.
Trees join in with rustling cheer,
Turning timber into fun atmosphere.

Chorus of the Greenery

Every twig plays a silly tune,
As sunlight dances, none too soon.
Leaves twirl in a chaotically fun,
While vines play tag, just on the run.

A rogue pinecone drops with a thud,
Shouting to the ground with a little mud.
Nuts and berries join in with glee,
The forest bursts in playful spree.

Whims of the Woodlands

In the woodlands, laughter rings,
From shy rabbits sporting spring things.
Bamboo poles tap dance with delight,
As the fireflies weave a sparkly flight.

Frogs on lilypads form a band,
Croaking out rhythms, simply grand.
Along comes a fox, with a wag of his tail,
Joining the fun with a comical wail.

Untold Stories of Saplings

In the garden, whispers grow,
Little saplings, stealing the show.
With their roots all tangled tight,
They wrestle worms, a funny sight.

Tiny leaves in sunlit dance,
A breeze nudges them to prance.
"Look at me!" they seem to shout,
While shadows tease them all about.

Chasing bugs with giddy glee,
What a wild and wacky spree!
One claims that it's quite a feat,
To outgrow the neighbor's sweet beet.

As seasons change, their tales unfold,
Each one prouder, each one bold.
With laughter ringing through the air,
Little saplings, beyond compare.

Contrast of Calm and Chaos

Amidst the trees, a squirrel twirls,
While down below, a leaf unfurls.
One whispers soft, the other leaps,
In nature's play, the laughter sweeps.

The wind rustles with a sly grin,
While sunshine plays violin.
Roots hold firm, but branches sway,
Inviting chaos into the fray.

A bird dodges, with a cheeky tweet,
While mushrooms jiggle with dainty feet.
Under calm skies, the dance won't cease,
In this garden, the fun's a feast!

Embrace the jests that life can brew,
In lively greens, and skies so blue.
It's chaos wrapped in serene charm,
Nature's laugh, a secret balm.

The Art of Arboreal Silence

Trees stand tall with regal grace,
In their shades, we find our place.
Whispers flutter, but can't be seen,
As branches chuckle, calm and keen.

Beneath the still, a laughter stirs,
Roots whisper tales, just like purrs.
With every rustle, stories brew,
In arboreal silence, giggles too.

Mighty oaks, with wisdom bold,
Share secrets that never grow old.
Yet on a whim, they sway and joke,
With branches that play, no need to poke.

Leaves swing gently on summer's breeze,
Nature's jesters, intent to tease.
In silent mirth, each tree takes flight,
Creating joy, a pure delight.

Ambient Echoes of Nature

Echoes linger, soft and sweet,
Where nature's laughter finds its beat.
Bouncing off the trunks so wide,
In this symphony, we abide.

The frogs croak tunes, a wobbly sound,
As breezes carry them all around.
Crickets chirp with rhythmic flair,
An orchestra beneath the air.

Sunbeams dance on flowing streams,
While flowers open, chasing dreams.
Insects hum a funny song,
With buzzing notes, they can't go wrong.

Breath of nature, humor's cheer,
In every rustle, laughter near.
An ambient joy that intertwines,
With the heartbeat of the pines.

The Language of the Woods

The trees are chatting, it's quite absurd,
A squirrel took notes, like he's heard a word.
They whisper of acorns, and secrets untold,
Beneath swaying branches, mysteries unfold.

The leaves tell jokes, as they dance in the breeze,
While mushrooms giggle, a real fungi tease.
A bark-bench confesses, with humor so dry,
In this leafy world, even shadows can sigh.

Old stumps are wise, they have stories to share,
Of woodland parties, and critters' affair.
They chuckle of owls who hoot out of tune,
In the grand comedy script that nature attunes.

So if you walk softly, just lend them an ear,
The forest is laughing, it's feeling quite queer.
With nature's own language, all humans can see,
That even the woods love a good chuckle spree.

Roots That Bind Us

Underneath the soil, a root party thrives,
They mingle and wiggle, as each root arrives.
A beetle's the DJ, spinning tunes underground,
While the plants sway gently, they dance all around.

Sharing their gossip, those roots intertwine,
"Did you hear about Clover? She's growing just fine!"
"Last week I tripped over a stone in the mud,
But thank goodness, friends, I just turned into bud!"

In their underground meetings, they've got quite a plan,
To tickle the groundhogs, and confound the man.
They laugh at the weather, come rain or come shine,
Rooted together, they know they will dine.

So next time you walk, through the soil and the grass,
Remember the roots, having fun as they pass.
With a wink and a wiggle, they cheerfully bind,
These roots of our lives, so hilariously intertwined.

Symphony of the Seasons

Spring springs with laughter, as flowers bloom bright,
They giggle and wiggle, what a colorful sight!
Bees buzz in chorus, such a busy delight,
While raindrops, like dancers, put on quite the flight.

Summer strolls in, with a sunburnt grin,
Tickling the leaves, as the fun does begin.
Picnics and laughter, the ice cream drips down,
While crickets perform in their summer-night gown.

Autumn arrives, with a rustle and cheer,
"Who's wearing those colors?" the trees laugh and jeer.
They play hide-and-seek with the falling gold leaves,
While squirrels wear acorns, the best of their sleeves.

Winter rolls in, a cold frosty friend,
The trees start to shiver, but they don't need to bend.
With snowflakes like confetti, they chuckle in chill,
The seasons are playful, and nature's the thrill.

The Heartbeat of the Forest

In the forest's core, there's a rhythm so sly,
With critters and creatures, it catches your eye.
A rabbit's quick hop, a turtle's slow lag,
Together they pulse, like a well-kept tag.

The heartbeat's loud laughter, it echoes around,
As the fox tries to dance, with no feet on the ground.
With trees as the choir, they sing through the night,
A cacophony of giggles, so silly yet bright.

The owls tell tall tales, while the beavers just grin,
"Why did the tree fall? It couldn't find its kin!"
Each creature plays part, in this whimsical play,
Life's rhythm is funny, it'll brighten your day.

So listen quite closely, to the forest's loud cheer,
In its heartbeat, there's joy, no need for a fear.
It's a laugh-out-loud masterpiece, wild and untamed,
Join in the fun, you'll never be blamed.

Forests of Forgotten Songs

In the woods where squirrels play,
Old tunes drift and sway.
Each branch holds a giggle tight,
As owls hoot with all their might.

The pines whisper silly tales,
Of baked acorns and fishy gales.
The leaves dance in laughing glee,
As rabbits hum in harmony.

A raccoon strums a leafy harp,
While frogs croak like a vibrant lark.
The forest is a merry mess,
Of joyful sound, no need to stress.

Beneath the moon's cheeky grin,
The jolly forest folks begin.
With laughter ringing in the night,
They sing till dawn's first light.

The Silent Symphony

In a world where whispers roam,
The trees have found a home.
Their leaves, a rustling choir,
Singing songs that never tire.

A shy root plays a muted bass,
While shadows join the silly race.
The breeze brings giggles on its trail,
As echoes dance, a happy wail.

Mushrooms tap their tiny toes,
In a concert no one knows.
Grass blades sway in comic time,
Creating beats that rhyme and chime.

Even the rocks can't help but grin,
As nature's jesters start to spin.
A silent show for all to share,
In the forest light, without a care.

Nature's Narrative

The sun wakes up to tell a tale,
Of wily snakes and a feathered snail.
A chipmunk writes with acorn ink,
While butterflies pause to blink.

A family of frogs plot a heist,
To snatch flies sweetened with honeyed ice.
The leaves flutter as if to cheer,
For every joke that they can hear.

An old tree knows all the tricks,
With roots so deep, it feels the kicks.
Branches sway in riotous glee,
As nature laughs whimsically.

Underneath the sky so wide,
Flora and fauna join the ride.
In tales both silly and profound,
The humor of nature knows no bound.

The Emissaries of Evergreen

In the land of sprightly green,
Evergreens plot a comical scene.
With pine cones as their little hats,
They giggle softly, like playful cats.

The cedars hold an acrobat show,
As critters leap to and fro.
The lichen paints a cheeky pose,
With giggles whispered on the nose.

In the midst of the needle dance,
Nature takes a friendly chance.
With every breeze, a chuckle flies,
Bringing joy as the sun does rise.

So let's raise a glass to the trees,
Who always know how to tease.
In their green embrace, we find delight,
With laughter echoing through the night.

The Melody of the Gnarled Heartwood

In the forest, full of trees,
A squirrel danced, doing the freeze.
With acorns hidden, raised on high,
He wore a hat, oh my, oh my!

Beneath the branches, shadows played,
A bear tried yoga, then he swayed.
The owl hooted, guiding him,
In a forest groove, they danced on whim.

The roots wore shoes, a sight to see,
Swinging vines made all agree.
Every leaf joined in with glee,
Nature's laughter, wild and free!

So bring your friends, let's join the fun,
With giggles echoing, everyone!
In every inch this life's a spree,
Together we're the best of three!

Ode to the Green Guardians

The trees wore glasses, wise and neat,
Taking notes on how we eat.
"Is that a twig or tasty snack?"
We paused a bit, then took it back!

A raccoon wore a chef's tall hat,
Cooking up a wild tree rat.
With tiny forks and tiny glee,
Served by a bird, all fancy-free!

The whispers spoke of leafly tea,
Made from twigs and honeybee.
"Try the bark, it's rather great!"
Said the hedgehog, full of fate.

So toast your friend, let laughter flow,
With giggles bouncing, fast and slow.
These green guardians say it's clear,
Life tastes better when you cheer!

Whispers of the Grove

In the grove, leaves flipped and twirled,
The trees chatted, their stories whirled.
A twig said, "Why did the branch go?"
"To get to the other side, you know!"

The critters laughed, they rolled in mirth,
"Why be sad when joy has worth?"
With playful hops and flappy wings,
They made up songs about silly things.

A ladybug wore polka-dot lace,
Practicing her dance, just in case.
The beetles clapped, oh what a sight,
As fireflies lit up the night!

So gather 'round, let's have a cheer,
Nature's joy is always near.
In leafy tunes, let's find our groove,
In giggles, we all find the mood!

The Song of the Silvan Spirits

In the glade where shadows play,
Silly spirits came out to sway.
They juggled mushrooms, oh what fun,
While mushrooms danced, their day begun.

A fox in boots and spiffy coat,
Rode a turtle, oh what a quote!
"Life's a journey, slow or fast,
Laugh it up, let the good times last!"

The clouds above joined in the chase,
Dropping raindrops, splashing grace.
Every tree shrugged off the rain,
"Plenty of water, let's dance again!"

So raise a cup to leafy friends,
In every cackle, joy transcends.
These silvan spirits hum along,
With nature's pulse, we all belong!

Underneath the Wildwood

Underneath the wildwood, a squirrel hopped,
With acorns galore, it never stopped.
A bird on a branch gave a loud caw,
Claiming the best seat, much to my awe.

The rabbits threw parties, all dressed in style,
While foxes played poker, laughing awhile.
A hedgehog rolled in, all covered in leaves,
Claiming to win, though no one believes.

The mushrooms held meetings, in circles they sat,
Discussing the weather, a serious chat.
But with every poke, they wept from the giggles,
For toadstool diplomacy involves silly wiggles.

So next time you wander where trees do confide,
Remember the antics that happen inside.
For underneath the wildwood, all creatures agree,
Life's a banquet of laughter, come join us for tea!

The Dance of Leaves and Light

The leaves spun around, in a wild ballet,
With a rustling giggle, they danced through the day.
Sunbeams were spotlights, so bright and so warm,
While squirrels were dancers in a charming swarm.

A wise old oak cheered, with a creaky old voice,
As the critters around him rejoiced in their choice.
They flipped and they twirled, with no hint of a care,
While shadows played tag in the sun-soaked air.

Dandelions chimed in, with a swaying refrain,
And butterflies giggled, caught up in the chain.
The moon peeked down, with a grin on its face,
Murmuring, "What fun! I'd join if I could race!"

So twirl with the leaves, let your worries take flight,
Join the merry band in this vibrant light.
For nature's a stage, and you've got a role,
In the dance of the leaves, just follow your soul!

Pines in Poetic Reverie

The pines struck a pose, like a bossy ballet,
With needles like fingers, they swayed to the play.
They whispered sweet nothings to the breeze by the lake,
While the sun took a role, for warmth's gentle sake.

A woodpecker chimed in, with his loud little tap,
Announcing their meeting—"No time for a nap!"
The squirrels wore ties, the rabbits donned shoes,
In a fashion parade that would make the news!

The pinecones debated if they should join in,
Saying, "We're too prickly, oh dear, where's the win?"
But the bushes just laughed, all fluffy and bold,
"Join us, dear friends, don't let fun grow cold!"

So here in the grove, under skies oh so wide,
Pines swirl in a dream, with nature as guide.
In this whimsical place, there's always a chance,
To join in the fun, and enjoy the sweet dance!

Rituals of the Rooted

Down in the forest, where roots intertwine,
The trees hold their meetings, engaging in whine.
"Who stole my sunlight?!" a willow did shout,
As mushrooms chimed in, "Let's wiggle it out!"

The ferns wore green gowns, with a fluttering grace,
While lizards held court, claiming prime space.
A rabbit brought snacks, but forgot the carrots,
So acorns were shared by the wise elder ferrets.

The fox brought a tale, of a missing ruffed cat,
While everyone gasped, and then giggled at that.
With laughter like echoes, they spun tales so tall,
About how they'd catch him, besting them all!

So next time you wander where roots dive so deep,
Remember the stories that nature will keep.
For in rituals of laughter, with friends by your side,
Life's quirks are the treasures where all hearts abide!

Nature's Timeless Chime

In the forest, trees do sway,
Chatting leaves, come out to play.
Branches wiggle, birds all sing,
Nature's laughter is the thing.

Squirrels plot with crafty schemes,
Hiding nuts, or so it seems.
They giggle hard, then change their route,
Laughing loud, they're on the lookout.

Sunlight peeks through leafy crowns,
Casting shadows on the ground.
A breeze tickles, whispers tease,
Nature's joke, that's sure to please.

In this realm where critters play,
Life's a joke in its own way.
So let us join their merry dance,
In this leafy, wild expanse.

Secrets of the Shaded Realm

Beneath the boughs where shadows creep,
Trees hold secrets, ancient, deep.
Rabbits hop while owls just stare,
Laughing softly at the air.

Mossy carpets, a sneaky trap,
Swaying roots that take a nap.
While the crickets chirp and tease,
The breeze joins in, bent on a spree.

The mushrooms wear their polka dots,
Hiding tales of all the plots.
Foxes grin with cunning flair,
Nature's theater is laid bare.

Twisted vines like a sly embrace,
Each leaf a smile, a cheeky face.
In the shade, we laugh and roam,
In this green and leafy home.

The Voice of the Verdant

Whispers rise in leafy dells,
Trees gossip like old chums, oh well!
A woodpecker's tap, join the beat,
Nature's band can't be beat.

Frogs croak jokes along the way,
While beetles dance, it's a bug ballet.
The wind shares tales from distant shores,
As nature's laughter often soars.

The flowers giggle, bright and bold,
Their colors dance, a sight to behold.
In this green world, humor's prime,
The trees can't help but chime!

From high above to below the moss,
Nature's antics can be a toss.
Join the fun, don't just abide,
Let the plants be your guide!

Harmony in the Helix

In spirals of leaves, stories unfold,
Twisty tales, both silly and bold.
The wind whirls laughter, round and round,
In this silly dance, joy's found.

Caterpillars in a conga line,
Wiggling along like they're feeling fine.
Each wiggle's a giggle, a twist and a turn,
Nature's rhythm makes our hearts yearn.

The daisies chuckle with the bees,
While ants march home, as if to tease.
Twigs and sticks break out in song,
In this forest, nothing can go wrong.

With each new dawn, the fun begins,
From morning light to evening spins.
Together we laugh, together we sway,
In nature's embrace, come what may!

The Call of the Canopy

In the shade of the branches, I found a small squirrel,
He danced with the leaves, giving nature a twirl.
With acorns as maracas, he crafted a tune,
A concert of chaos beneath the bright moon.

A bee buzzed along, wearing tiny bowed glasses,
It joined in the fun, through flowers it passes.
Together they sang, the creatures took flight,
While I laughed at their antics, what a silly sight.

A wise old oak gave a chuckle with glee,
"Why don't you join in? It's as fun as can be!"
I shrugged and I swayed to their rhythmic delight,
In the choir of the trees, I danced through the night.

As the stars blinked above, a raccoon took a dive,
With his fork and his jest, he felt so alive.
So let's raise a toast to the happy old tree,
For the loud, laughable life that grows wild and free.

Shadows Singing Softly

Under the sprawling branches, where shadows do play,
The breezes are giggling, they sweep smiles away.
A leaf tried to flutter but tripped on a twig,
It landed with flair in a dance so big.

The sun threw a spotlight on a frog in a coat,
He croaked his own ballad while on a small boat.
The bubbles were popping like popcorn in air,
And I couldn't stop snickering; it was all quite rare.

In the midst of the laughter, a butterfly flapped,
With wings made of polka dots, brightly enwrapped.
It twirled and it whirled, like a shirt on a line,
While shadows all giggled, "This party's divine!"

So if you're ever sad and need some cheer here,
Just visit the shadows, where silliness steers.
For in every soft whisper, and every light clap,
Are the echoes of laughter that give us a nap.

The Ethereal Essence of Elms

Among the ancient elms, where humor is born,
A jester of a jay began to adorn.
He wore a small hat made of twigs and a grin,
As he juggled some acorns, let the games begin.

With whispers of wisdom, the branches would sigh,
"I'm just here for the fun, so don't let it pass by!"
A breeze carried laughter—it tickled my ear,
As the elms shared their secrets, murmurings clear.

A hedgehog rolled by, dressed in glitter so bold,
With a cape made of moss, he looked quite controlled.
He bounded and tumbled, his laughter a song,
In the essence of elms, we all danced along.

So here in this haven of giggles and mirth,
The elms gave us joy and a little rebirth.
Let the jokes keep on soaring, like leaves in a storm,
In the heart of this forest, we'll always keep warm.

Whispering Willows

In a grove of willows, where whispers do sway,
A group of small critters had come out to play.
With winks and with nudges, they'd skedaddle around,
While the branches bent low, adding giggles to sound.

A turtle on roller skates rolled right by my foot,
He exclaimed with a chuckle, "Try my newest route!"
With every slip and slide, he spread joy in the air,
The willows all shivered, their laughter to share.

The wind held a party, inviting us all,
With twirls and with giggles, we danced till the fall.
Each tree shared a tale as the sun slid away,
With their stories of laughter, in shadows we'd stay.

So next time you wander where the willows weave,
Remember the joy that the trees can achieve.
Join in the fun, leave your worries with glee,
For nature's a jester, just wait and see!

Tales Under Twisted Limbs

Beneath the branches wide and low,
Squirrels gossip fast with quite a show.
One drops an acorn, oh what a clatter,
While folks below just laugh and chatter.

A raccoon dines on berries sweet,
Wearing a hat made of green beet.
The trees they giggle, rustling leaves,
As mischief dwells among the eaves.

A bird sings loud, so off key,
The owl rolls eyes, quite snooty, you see.
But every laugh from bark to bark,
Keeps life so bright, igniting spark.

So gather round, come hear the tale,
Of woodland fables where giggles prevail.
With every breeze through twig and leaf,
Laughter thrives, beyond belief.

The Weaving of Woods

In twisted twigs, the stories flow,
Of woodland critters, don't you know?
A rabbit prances, a jaunty hop,
While squirrels bake cakes and never stop.

The pines lean close, a curious crowd,
As hedgehogs hum, so merry and loud.
They spin a yarn with playful flair,
Telling secrets the trees lay bare.

A chipmunk dressed in formal wear,
Danced on a stump with nary a care.
The force of fun, it's quite the show,
Woodland wonders in a breezy flow.

So let's not forget the giggles bright,
That echo through the woods at night.
From trees to critters, laughter ignites,
In the heart of woods, joy ignites.

Vignettes of Verdure

In fields of green with splatters of fun,
Where daisies spin under the sun.
A turtle tripped, what a silly scene,
With grass stains on his shell so green.

The daisies play hopscotch on the ground,
While a frog croaks out the funniest sound.
The trees shake limbs, they're tickled pink,
As nature's band starts to clink.

Bumbling bees in a dance so wild,
Bring honey home to a giggling child.
With every splash of color bold,
The story of woods begins to unfold.

So march along through vibrant glades,
Where laughter lives and never fades.
We'll find the fun in every leaf,
Amongst the trees, our shared belief.

Note of the Noble Trees

Oh noble trees, with tales so grand,
You whisper secrets with every strand.
There's a beaver planning a dance tonight,
With branches bobbing, oh what a sight!

The oak brings out its polka dots,
While willows sway, singing funny plots.
A gopher juggles acorns tossed,
Laughter echoes, never lost.

With every rustle, there's humor afoot,
As nature's critters strut and hoot.
The mushrooms join the jovial spree,
Twirling about, "Look at me!"

So here's to trees, evergreen and wise,
Their many notes bring joy to the skies.
Join in the frolic, let's collectively cheer,
For every branch, there's laughter here.

www.ingramcontent.com/pod-product-compliance
Lightning Source LLC
Chambersburg PA
CBHW071830160426
43209CB00003B/270